Play the Game

Karate

Play the Game

Karate

Karl Oldgate

WARD LOCK

Half-title page: *The front jab (Kizami-zuki) is an effective way to open the opponent's defence*

Title page: *A successful roundhouse kick (Mawashi-geri) depends not only on good twisting of the hips but also on lifting the knee high before execution of the kick*

Above: *The roundhouse kick to the face requires perfect balance, with your trunk at right angles to the standing leg*

Contents

Introduction

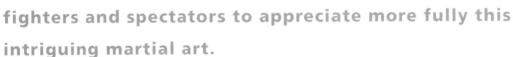

Interest in karate has been growing apace during the second half of the twentieth century, and here at last is a chance for fighters and spectators to appreciate more fully this intriguing martial art.

Play the Game: Karate gives the expert as well as the newcomer to karate a clear and broad insight into this exciting art. It explains the history and development of karate as well as giving a comprehensive picture of how *shotokan* – one of the most popular styles of karate – is practised today.

The sport of karate is presented here in a form at once attractive and understandable. In particular, the explanation of traditional karate practice and the translation of the phraseology are quite thorough and will help the new student to pick up the 'extras' which always accompany the learning of this sport.

The book 'scores' in that it not only explains how the

technique is performed but also goes on to show how techniques are applied in numerous situations. Anyone thinking of entering competitions will benefit greatly from studying the fighting strategies described in these pages.

Karate is not easy to learn. It requires concentration and hard work. But for anyone who is prepared to make the effort, the results can be surprising. Many people who thought they had no aptitude for karate have found that they have become proficient, and they enjoy the fitness and comradeship which comes from being a member of a karate club.

This book is therefore recommended as a useful accompaniment to the practical training in a club approved by the official governing body of karate.

History & development of karate

Karate, which literally means 'empty hand', comes in many different forms as you will see when you read through this book. But it all stems from the fifth century AD and a Zen Buddhist priest called Bhodidharma.

In those days priests were experts at self-defence because they were constantly battling (literally!) against parishioners of differing faiths. Their self-defence was based on yoga techniques.

Towards the end of the fifth century Bhodidharma went from India to China to teach at the Shaolin-Szu monastery where he taught his pupils the yoga techniques necessary to bring together the enlightenment of both body and soul. However, he found the exercise too strenuous for his students, and in an effort to build up their stamina he introduced a form of Chinese fighting called *kempo* into their training schedule. It worked, and soon the Shaolin-Szu Temple became one of the most respected fighting schools in China.

Kempo was used alongside medicine techniques of the day and various vital parts of the body were pinpointed for medical science which the Chinese used in acupuncture. These target areas were used as areas of attack in *kempo* and later formed the basis for attack areas of karate.

Although the Shaolin-Szu techniques soon spread throughout China, it was being practised with local variations of the basic technique in various parts of the country. The techniques were soon carried to neighbouring countries and across waters to nearby islands. One such island to benefit from the Shaolin-Szu style of combat was Okinawa, the main island in the Ryukyu chain which stretches from Japan to Taiwan.

Okinawa had already had its own form of combat for many years before the arrival of the Shaolin-Szu technique. It was known simply as *te* which meant hand and was a form of unarmed combat which made full use of the hands.

Te had fallen into disuse as warriors started carrying weapons. But in the late fifteenth century the *te* form of fighting received a boost when restrictions on the use and carrying of arms were imposed on Okinawa's residents. When *kempo* reached Okinawa, the Japanese own style of fighting *(te)* combined with the Chinese form to create *Tang Hand*.

However, the word karate was only eventually adopted in the twentieth century. In 1922 (Gichin) Funakoshi, an Okinawan exponent of *Tang Hand*, was invited to give a demonstration in Japan. He had combined some of the skills of *te*, *Tang Hand* and the Japanese *Ju-jitsu* to create a new form of fighting. Funakoshi called the new form 'karate' and wrote: 'As a mirror's polished surface reflects whatever stands before it and a quiet valley carries even small sounds, so must the student of karate render his mind empty of selfishness in an effort to react appropriately towards anything he might encounter.' This is the meaning of 'kara' in karate and remains one of the principle concepts – the emptying of the mind of all thoughts.

Funakoshi therefore allied the form of combat to that of Zen Buddhism of the fifth century. Zen was the meditation aspect of karate, while karate was the action element.

Funakoshi's style of karate was known as *shotokan* (so named because his nickname was Shoto) and it was to be the forerunner of other styles which developed – *shitoryu, gojuryu, wadoryu, shukokai* and *kyokushinkai.*

Shotokan is the most popular style of karate practised worldwide. In Britain, it is by far the most prominent martial art, represented by numerous organizations. The original, and still the largest, is the Karate Union of Great Britain (KUGB), the only *shotokan* group recognized by the Japan Karate Association (JKA). The KUGB was established in 1966 shortly after the arrival from Japan of two of the JKA's most famous instructors, Hirokozu Kanazawa and Keinosuke Enoeda. In 1968, Kanazawa resigned from the KUGB to become chief instructor for Germany and so it was Enoeda and chief British instructor Andy Sherry who were to oversee the development of the KUGB. Throughout thirty years of growth and success in top-level competition both in the UK and abroad, the KUGB has gained international respect. Although having never been a member of the World Union of Karate-do Organizations (WUKO) – the world governing body – and despite being an ex-member of the English Karate Governing Body, the KUGB continues to be recognized as a highly technical organization, promoting the highest standards to be found anywhere in karate. It has produced a great many respected instructors, who themselves have enjoyed competitive careers over many years – the most famous being Frank Brennan.

As for the other styles of karate, *shitoryu* was founded by Kenwa Mabuni who took his style to Japan in 1930. Chojun Miyagi, like Mabuni and Funakoshi, hailed from Okinawa, and took his style *gojuryu* to Japan. Although born in Okinawa he lived in China for many years and studied *kempo*. He was an expert at 'in-fighting'.

Hironori Ohtsuka was a Japanese student of *ju-jitsu* at Waseda University, and adopted karate techniques of *ju-jitsu* to form the *wadoryu* (Way of Peace) school of karate. Another Japanese student, Chojiro Tani, founded the *shukokai* (Way for All) school which emphasizes speed and movement. A former student of Mabuni, he broke away to form his own school in 1950.

Another major style of karate is *kyokushinkai* (The Peak of Truth) which was founded by the Korean Masutatsu Oyama. As a fifteen-year-old in 1938 he went to Japan to study aviation. To strengthen his self-discipline he lived a life of solitude in the mountains for two years and he is also famous for having fought bulls unarmed!

There are other techniques, like *wadokai, gojukai, shotokai, kanshinryu,* and the Chinese *kung-fu* kicking and punching form which was popularized by martial artist/actor Bruce Lee. *Wing-chun* was another system used by Lee. But the five schools as outlined are the ones regarded as the principle styles of karate.

Because each style was at first unique, the possibility of competition between rival exponents was impossible, and indeed unthinkable. Their style and techniques are so individual that respective schools took all precautions to make sure 'outsiders' did not get a look at their training schedules (*katas*).

Because of the high level of European and American servicemen in Japan during the Second World War, many became fans of one form or another of karate and some took what they had learnt back to their respective countries. It helped to spread the karate word worldwide but there still remained so many different styles that international competition was impossible. However, in 1964, in an effort to formulate a standardized set of rules, the Federation of All Japan Karate-do Organizations (FAJKO) was formed with state approval. But progress was slow and it was not until 1970, when other national associations had started springing up, that the first 'all styles' world championship was organized and held in Tokyo. At the same time a meeting was held and a world governing body, the World Union of Karate-do Organizations (WUKO), was established.

The British association had been established in 1967 and when members went to Paris for the second world championship in 1972 they became the first country team to beat Japan in international competition. Since then, Great Britain has become one of the world's leading karate nations with fighters such as Wayne Otto and Molly Samuels winning world individual titles, in WUKO events.

Equipment &
terminology

Before learning how to practise karate, it is important to familiarize yourself with the equipment needed, and the terminology you will come across as you get to grips with the game.

(While it is fully appreciated that many women and girls participate in karate, for simplicity all references to *karateka* are in the male form. This isn't chauvinism … just a case of making the text a bit clearer!)

EQUIPMENT

Getting started in karate is not all that expensive. You can start by wearing a track suit, which you will probably have anyway. But if you want to buy a karate suit *(karategi)* then it will cost anything between £20 and £100.

The suit is white but, unlike a judo suit, is light-fitting. It should not have any coloured piping or identification marks on it. The jacket must be long enough to cover the hips. Women may wear a plain white T-shirt under their jacket. The sleeves of the jacket must come at least half way down the forearm, and the trouser legs must cover at least two-thirds of the shin. To prevent perspiration dripping into your eyes a head band *(hachimaki)* can be worn, but not in a *kumite* contest. Like judo, shoes are not worn when performing a *kata* or in a competitive contest.

The jacket of the suit is tied with a belt which, like other martial arts, is of varying colour depending upon a fighter's level of skill. The belt system varies according to karate style but all styles have Kyu (student) and Dan (senior) grades. The following is an example of a typical belt grading system, starting with the least experienced to most experienced of fighters.

Novice – white
6th Kyu – red
5th Kyu – yellow
4th Kyu – orange
3rd Kyu – green
2nd Kyu – blue
1st Kyu – brown
1st–10th Dan – black

The fully attired karateka *in his* karategi *and wearing regulation mitts*

All Dans are black belts and it is very rare to find a fighter of a higher grade than 3rd/4th Dan. If a *karateka* attains 8th Dan status he has the option to wear a red belt during class, which shows he has completed his full circle of learning from 6th Kyu to 6th Dan.

During competitive bouts one fighter wears a red belt and is referred to as *aka*. The other wears a white belt and he is referred to as *shiro*. Each fighter must also wear an identifying number on their backs.

You are not allowed to roll up the sleeves of your jacket or the legs of your trousers, and you must not wear a dirty *karategi*.

The World Union of Karate-do Organizations (WUKO) require competitors to wear white protective padded mitts. They must have no more than 1cm (⅜in) of padding and have an uncovered thumb. While karate in the modern-day form is also practised as a sport and is not intended to cause harm to its participants, accidents can happen and the wearing of these mitts is considered by WUKO to reduce the risk of such incidents.

Not all karate organizations endorse the wearing of mitts,

stitched finger-separator

max. 1cm
(⅜in) padding

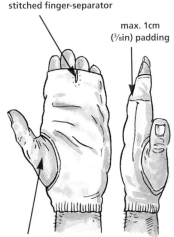

thumb is free
(no padding)

THE REGULATION MITTS
Dirty, torn or frayed mitts are not
allowed in tournament events

however, maintaining that medical evidence supports the view held by many *karateka* that they can actually encourage a lack of control. Very skilful *karateka* are able to control techniques with or without mitts, but less experienced competitors who lack skill or those who have little regard for the safety of their opponent may use 'protection' as an excuse to hit harder. Should your organization require you to wear mitts, you must exercise the same degree of control as when practising without 'safety' equipment.

Gumshields are compulsory and, for the men, a well-fitting jockstrap is also suggested as a vital piece of your karate attire.

The only other expense you will incur will be in joining a club and/or paying for lessons. Membership fees vary according to the club, but it is advisable to ensure that you join a reputable club that is affiliated to an established and respected official body. Unfortunately the situation still persists in which some inadequately qualified instructors are teaching poor karate in return for extortionate fees. You should pay no more than £3 for a regular club session and something in the region of £15 for an annual licence.

Because most karate practice does not involve throws, the fighting area does not need to be as padded as that for judo. In fact, an area as heavily padded as a judo mat would slow down a karate fighter. The mats should be of a non-slip type and have a low friction value on the upper surface.

The actual contest area should measure 8m (26ft) by 8m (26ft), and be made up of smaller mats. It is essential that a referee makes sure the mats do not separate during a contest because gaps can cause serious injury.

A 1m (3ft) safety area surrounds the 8m (26ft) contest area, and two markers at the centre of the area indicate where the fighters should take up position at the start, or re-start, of a contest. Fighters stand 2m (6ft 6in) apart at address. There should be no pillars, advertising hoardings, walls, or any other obstacle, within 1m (3ft) of the outer perimeter of the fighting area.

So that's karate equipment. As you can see it does not take a lot to get a contest under way. But to perfect the art takes many years of dedication and practice. You will also have to familiarize yourself with the numerous terms which are associated with karate, most of which are of Japanese origin.

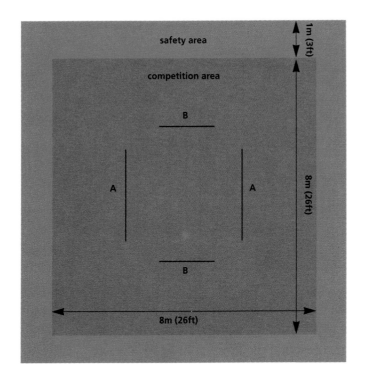

safety area

competition area

B

A   A

B

8m (26ft)

1m (3ft)

8m (26ft)

THE COMPETITION AREA
This can be elevated up to 1m (3ft) above the floor area but, if it is, there must be a safety area of at least 2m (6ft 6in) around the perimeter

A = competitor's lines
B = referee's/judge's lines

TERMINOLOGY

The following are a selection of terms that will crop up quite a lot when you are participating, whether it be in a contest or during practice.

Age-zuki A rising type of blow.

Ai-uchi The referee's call to indicate a simultaneous score which results in no points being awarded.

Aka The fighter designated the red belt in a *kumite*.

Ashi-barai A leg sweep.

Ashikubi Used in reference to the ankle or kicks made by a fighter with the ankle.

Ashi-no-achi-kata The ways of positioning the feet in readiness for an attacking or defensive move.

Ashiwaza Leg and foot techniques as used in kicking.

Atemi The vital points of the body.

Atoshi-baraku Audible call from the timekeeper to indicate 'a little more time left'. Normally given by the sounding of a bell or buzzer with 30 seconds remaining.

Awasette-ippon The score of two *waza-aris* added together to make one *ippon*.

Chakugan The correct focus of attention in a *kata*.

Choku zuki A straight punch.

Chudan The mid-section of the body, one of the key target areas.

Chudan-mawashi-geri The roundhouse kick to the mid-section.

Chusoku Contact point – the ball of the foot.

Dachi Stance.

Dan A senior grade – a black belt.

Dojo Karate club or training hall.

Encho-sen An extension to a karate contest, started with the referee calling *'shobu hajime'*.

Fudotachi A posture adopted by the *karateka* with feet wide apart, knees bent, and in a sideways position to the opponent.

Fukushin The judge in a *kumite* contest.

Fumikeri A stamping or slicing sideways kick.

Gargu-kamae Known as the 'reclining dragon' stance. Vital parts of the body are protected by turning away from the opponent.

Gedan The body below the waist.

Gedan barai A downward sweeping block.

Geri A kick.

Gyaku-zuki The reverse punch.

Haisoku Contact point – the instep.

Hajime The referee's call to 'begin'.

Hansoku Loss of a contest by a disqualification, from e.g. a foul.

Hansoku-chui A penalty award of an *ippon* to your opponent.

Hantei The referee's call for the judges to make a decision.

Hanteigachi A win by a decision.

Heraite A sweeping hand method of defence against an attack by your opponent's hand or foot.

Hiraken Contact point – the half-clenched fist. The contact points are the second joints of the index and middle fingers.

Hikiwake A drawn contest.

Hitosashiyubi-ipponken Contact point – the knuckle joint of the index finger.

Hiza The knee.

Hizagashira The knee-cap.

Hiza-geri An attack made with the knee-cap.

Hizatsui An attack on the vital parts of your opponent's body with the knee-cap.

Ibuki A method of breathing involving the tensing of all muscles after inhaling.

Ippon A full point, which is the highest score in karate. The referee will award it if a blow is delivered to one of the defined areas of the opponent's body with the correct posture and stance, from the correct distance, and with spirit and good focus.

Jion A *Shotokan kata*; named after a temple.

Jiu-kumite Freestyle fighting.

Jodan The head area.

Jodan-zuki A punch delivered to the head area.

Jogai Exit from the fighting area.

Kakato Contact point – the heel.

Kakato-geri A kick with the heel.

Kakiwake A defensive action using a thrusting hand to sweep away an opponent's wrist.

Kansa The arbitrator in a *kumite* contest.

Karategi The karate suit. Often referred to as the '*gi*'.

Karateka A person who practises karate.

Kata A fixed sequence of training exercises which incorporate aspects of attack and defence and takes the form of imaginary fighting.

Keage A snapping action.

The various stances are designed for specific purposes. Those with a low centre of gravity and a wide foot stance are ideal for powerful punching

Keiko Contact point – the fingertips and thumb.

Keikoku A penalty award of a *waza-ari* to your opponent.

Kekomi A thrusting action.

Keriage An upwards kick using either the sole of the foot or front of the ankle.

Keriwaza Kicking techniques.

Kiai The shout given out by the *karateka* as he executes a technique with maximum power and spirit.

Kihon Basic technical training and fighting forms.

Kizami-zuki Front hand jab.

Koken Contact point – the wrist.

Kokutsu-dachi One of the basic stances – the back stance.

Kote The forearm.

Kumite A contest or match.

Kyoshi A very high master, normally of 6th, 7th or 8th Dan.

Kyu A student.

Mae-geri The front kick.

Makiwara A padded board or bag used for punching and kicking training exercises.

Mawashi-zuki The roundhouse punch.

Moto-no-ichi The call for the contestants, referee and judge to return to their respective standing lines.

Mubobi When one, or both, fighters displays a lack of regard for his own safety.

Nakayubi-ipponken Contact point – the second joint of the middle finger.

Nidan A 2nd Dan.

Nukite Contact point – the fingertips or spearhand.

Obi Another name for the coloured belt worn by *karateka*.

Rei The traditional bow by each *karateka* to each other before and after a contest.

Renshi Senior expert grades, normally applied to 4th or 5th Dans. *Renshi* grade *karateka* are entitled to be called *sensei* (honourable teacher) by their juniors.

Sagi-ashi-dachi Known as the 'Heron Leg' posture because the *karateka* raises one leg to a position approximately level with the knee of the supporting leg.

Sanbon-ippon A three-point *kumite* bout.

Sandan A 3rd Dan.

Seiken Contact point – the forefist.

Semete An attacking fighter in *kata*.

Sensei A term of respect from a junior to a *renshi*. It means 'honourable teacher'.

Shihan A term of respect by a junior for a *karateka* of 8th Dan or higher. It means 'honourable professor'.

Shikkaku Disqualification from a bout, match and competition for a serious breach of karate rules and/or regulations.

Shiro The wearer of the white belt in a *kumite* contest.

A fighter on guard, ready to spring her defence when attacked

Shitei The compulsory section of a *kata* competition.

Shobu-ippon A one-point *kumite* bout.

Shodan A 1st Dan.

Shotei Contact point – the heel of the palm.

Shugo The beckoning of the judge by the referee.

Shushin The referee.

Shuto Contact point – the knife hand.

Sokuto Contact point – the knife foot.

Soremade The referee's call to indicate the contest is over.

Sukuite A scooping-hand, defensive technique in which you grasp your opponent's hand, leg or foot.

Tamashiwara The art of wood-breaking.

Te The hand.

Tegatana The hand-sword technique effected with the thumb turned into the palm and the fingers extended. The contact point is the bottom edge of the palm.

Tekubi The wrist.

Tetsui Contact point – the fist edge.

Tewaza Hand technique.

Tobigeri A spectacular jumping kick with both feet making the opponent uncertain with which foot the kick will be made.

Tokui The free selection part of a *kata* competition, or a *karateka*'s favourite *kata*.

Torimasen Call by the referee to indicate an unacceptable scoring technique.

Tsuki or **Zuki** A blow made with the closed hand, utilizing the forefist or *Seiken*.

Tsuzukete hajime The referee's call to 'fight on' after an interruption.

Ude The arm.

Uke A defensive action or block.

Uraken Contact point – the inverted (or back) fist.

Ushiro-geri The back kick or spinning back kick.

Ushiro-mawashi-geri A reverse roundhouse kick.

Waza-ari A half-point score awarded for a well-timed punch which does not fulfil the criteria for *ippon* but is nevertheless judged effective.

Yame! Referee's call to 'stop'.

Yoi Referee's call of 'ready'.

Yoko-geri A side kick.

Zanshin The state of continued awareness after a technique has landed. In other words, the fighter must be ready for a potential counter-attack from his opponent.

Zenkutsu-dachi One of the basic stances adopted by a *karateka*.

Zen-no Silent meditation.

The side kick (yoko-geri) requires good timing, balance and concentration to execute successfully

The game – a guide

The most common form of karate is a freestyle fighting known as *jiu-kumite*. The rules are basically straightforward.

You have various parts of your body with which you are allowed to attack your opponent, and there are certain parts of the body designated as target areas. To score points you have to carry out a technique which, in the referee's opinion, is good enough to carry a one-point score (an *ippon*) or a half-point score (a *waza-ari*). What could be simpler? The target areas are clearly defined and any other parts of your opponent's anatomy are outlawed. The target areas are: head; face; upper abdomen and stomach; chest; and back (excluding shoulders).

Karate contests take place on a square mat measuring 8m (26ft). A cross is marked at the centre of the mat. The bouts are controlled by a referee (*shushin*) and a judge (*fukushin*) who position themselves on the mat and should be opposite each other at all times. The sole decision rests with the referee who can consult his judge to make decisions. However, if he is undecided, then an arbitrator (*kansa*), who sits outside the contest area, is called upon to assist. There are also a timekeeper and scorer positioned outside the competition area.

The referee's role is to award points, take away points for fouls and generally to make sure the contest is run properly.

The two contestants wear identifying belts, normally one red *(aka)* and one white *(shiro)* at senior international level. These are worn instead of the belts a fighter wears to signify his grade.

Before a contest, the two competitors stand facing each other at the centre of the mat at a distance 2m (6ft 6in) apart and bow to each other. Upon the referee's call of *hajime* they start the contest. All calls are made in Japanese, hence the list of terms in the previous chapter.

The two fighters will spar by means of a free exchange of blows, blocks and counter-moves until one fighter gets a fully focused blow to one of the defined target areas. If successful, it is then up to the referee to decide if such a blow is a point-scoring *(ippon* or *waza-ari)* one.

The referee is looking for good-quality technique. For a blow to score points it must have good form, good attitude from the fighter, vigour, alertness, good timing, and be made from the ideal distance. If the referee sees a good technique delivered by one fighter he will call *yame* and the two fighters will return to their positions at the centre of the mat. The referee will then announce it

REFEREE'S SIGNALS (WUKO rules)

Hajime *(start)*

The signal to indicate a **waza-ari**

Above: *The signal to indicate an* ippon
Above right: *The signal to indicate*
Tsuzukete hajime *(resume fighting)*

as an *ippon* or *waza-ari*, to the appropriate fighter, and announce the type of point-scoring technique.

An *ippon* is a full point and is the maximum single score. To be awarded, the technique must hit the target area and be perfectly executed. Endeavour to take the opponent by surprise. This is one of the secrets of successful karate, being able to catch your opponent unaware. A score of three *ippon*s wins a bout.

If, in the referee's opinion the technique was good, but not good enough to warrant an *ippon* he will call a *waza-ari*, known as the half-point. It is normally awarded for a technique that hits the target area but has been partially blocked or not carried out with the perfection of the *ippon*. While a *waza-ari* is equivalent to 50 per cent of an *ippon* in terms of scoring, it is in fact equivalent to 90 per cent of an *ippon* in technical terms. So don't expect to get awarded a *waza-ari* for a half-perfected *ippon*.

When awarding points, the referee will be looking for *zanshin*, the part of a technique often missed or ignored when carrying out a move. *Zanshin* can be regarded as the state of continued commitment which continues after the technique has landed and should show the fighter maintaining concentration and awareness of the opponent's ability to counter-attack.

Penalty points are awarded for a wide variety of offences. A

The signal to indicate a Keikoku, a warning with a waza-ari penalty

fighter must not step out of the competition area. If he does, then the referee will call *jogai* to indicate a warning. If he steps out of the area a second time, a half-point penalty is awarded against him. If it happens again, a full point penalty is awarded and a fourth offence results in disqualification.

The signal to indicate a Hansoku-chui, a warning with an ippon penalty

The signal to indicate a foul

The signal to indicate shugo, the calling of the judge

Interruption or end of match which is accompanied by the referee's call of yame (stop fighting)

The signal to indicate hikiwake
(a draw)

If a technique is a non-scoring one, the referee will announce
torimasen *and make the above signals*

The signal to indicate a warning with
an ippon *penalty*

The signal to indicate jogai, *which means one (or both) fighter(s) has stepped outside the competition area*

The signal to indicate ai-uchi – a simultaneous technique from both fighters

A signal indicating that a fighter is receiving his 'marching orders' – in other words, a disqualification

The most common penalty points are those for illegal contacts. Kicks to the eyes, knees or groin are totally outlawed. Other areas of the body can be contacted with the hands or feet but must not be made with excessive force. Once you have found your way through your opponent's defence then you should hold back on the blow or kick. Striking your opponent with excessive force will carry penalty points.

The following is a list of prohibited behaviour as laid down in the rules of karate:

a. Techniques which make contact with the throat.

b. Techniques which make excessive contact.

c. Attacks to the groin, joints or instep.

d. Attacks to the face with an open hand technique.

e. Dangerous throws which will prevent your opponent from landing safely.

f. Techniques which, by their nature, cannot be controlled for the safety of your opponent.

g. Repeated direct attacks on your opponent's arms or legs.

h. Repeated exits from the competition area (as outlined above already).

i. Grappling, wrestling or violently pushing your opponent deliberately.

j. Any ungentlemanly behaviour.

k. Displaying a lack of regard for your own safety (known as *mubobi*).

l. Feigning injury in order to gain an advantage.

Following any infringement, the referee will either give a warning or award a penalty. The following scale of penalties will be awarded by the referee:

Keikoku Awarded for minor infractions for which a warning has already been given or for offences not serious enough to warrant a *hansoku-chui*. When awarding a *keikoku* a *waza-ari* is added to your opponent's score.

Hansoku-chui If this penalty is awarded against you, your opponent is credited with an *ippon*. It is normally awarded if a *keikoku* has already been awarded in the same bout.

FURTHER REFEREE SIGNALS (WUKO rules)

(A) Waza-ari
(B) Ippon
(C) Tarimasen *(no score)*
(D) Mienai *(I didn't see)*

A   B   C   D

(H) Warning
(I) Keikoku *(half-point penalty)*
(J) Hansoku-chui *(full-point penalty)*
(K) Hansoku *(foul)*

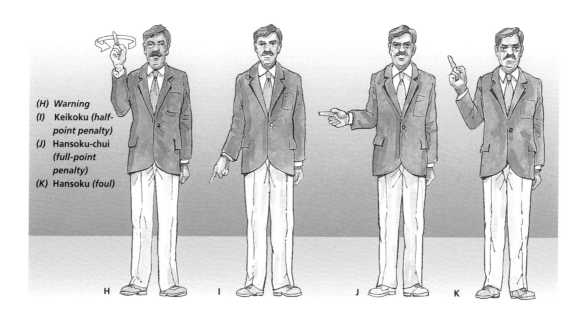

H   I   J   K

(E) Technique short of
    target
(F) Technique missed
    target
(G) Hikiwake *(draw)*

(L) Jogai *(exit from contest area)*
(M) Ai-uchi *(simultaneous score)*
(N) Excessive contact

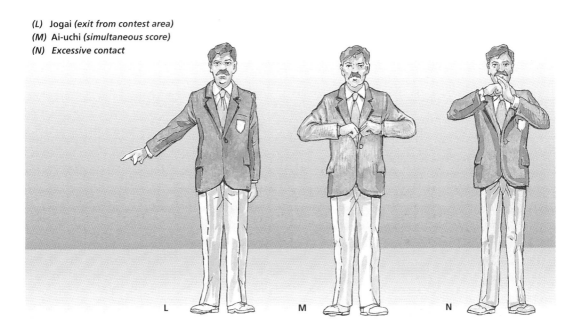

Hansoku The penalty awarded for a very serious breach of the rules and results in disqualification. The opponent's score is automatically raised to *sanbon* and he becomes the winner.

Shikkaku Disqualification from the entire tournament, competition or match following a very serious breach of the rules. The opponent's score will be raised to *sanbon*. Here are some reasons for the awarding of a *shikkaku*:

a. Harming the prestige and honour of karate.
b. Failing to obey the referee's orders.
c. Deliberately violating the rules regarding prohibited behaviour.
d. Jeopardising the smooth-running of a bout because of bad behaviour.

Because of the loose nature of the '*gi*' it is sometimes impossible, or certainly very difficult, for a referee to see whether the contact was excessive or not. On the other hand, there are some fighters who will exploit such a situation and feign injury so as to try and fool the referee into believing the blow was excessive. This is when you have to ask yourself whether you would fancy being a karate referee. The answer is probably no. His job is certainly a tough one so please accept his decision no matter whether you believe it to be right or wrong.

The length of a contest can vary according to the type of competition. But at senior level a men's contest will last three minutes while a women's or junior contest lasts two minutes. In certain circumstances contests can be extended to five minutes' duration, if the rules of the competition permit. The contest will end before then if one fighter has reached the required number of points, normally three. At the end of the contest the referee will order the two fighters back to their starting lines. He will take up his position and raise his hand on the side of the winner and announce *shiro* (or *aka*) *no kachi*. The bout is ended at this point.

In major international competitions fighters normally have to endure a series of elimination bouts on a straight knock-out basis until there are just two fighters left to contest the final. Contests can go into extra-time to decide a winner, again that depends on the rules of the competition.

Contests under WUKO rules take place between fighters within weight categories at senior level. The weight divisions are:

Men

Lightweight	– under 60kg (132lb)
Super-lightweight	– under 65kg (143lb)
Light-middleweight	– under 70kg (154lb)
Middleweight	– under 75kg (165lb)
Light-heavyweight	– under 80kg (176lb)
Heavyweight	– over 80kg (176lb)
Open class	– any

Women

Lightweight	– under 53kg (117lb)
Middleweight	– under 60kg (132lb)
Heavyweight	– over 60kg (132lb)

Now let's look at the rules of *kata*, the other most popular form of karate. *Kata* is a fixed sequence of basic defence and attack routines carried out without the aid of an opponent. It is designed for practice and takes the form of fighting imaginary attackers approaching from different directions. This form of 'practice' is played at competition level where a technically good routine is crucial. An experienced judge will readily see any flaw in the *karateka*'s technique. We will be looking at *kata* techniques later, but here are the rules affecting *kata* competitions.

First, a *kata* competition can be performed on a mat, but a polished wooden surface is better. It must obviously be free of splinters. There is no defined size of the area but it must be large enough to enable the *karateka* to carry out his routine. Dress is the standard *karategi* and the contestant wears his appropriate belt.

Competitions take the form of individual or team matches. In team events, three *karateka* constitute one team which must be either all-male or all-female. There are no mixed teams in WUKO events. Each contestant is required to perform a compulsory *(shitei)* routine and a free selection *(tokui)*.

A total of five judges will be designated for each match and they will be assisted by score-keepers and announcers.

A *kata* match is carried out on an elimination basis and after the first round of sequences the number of competitors is reduced to sixteen. After the second round it is reduced further to eight and the third round decides the final placings. If the same judges have officiated in all the rounds, the scores in all the rounds are aggregated. If a new set of judges is appointed for the final round, then only the points gained in the final round are counted. Each judge awards points for individual performances and displays the points allocated by holding up a card in his right hand. The maximum and minimum scores are not counted.

The judges are looking for the following points when making their assessment of a good routine:

a. It must be performed with competence and demonstrate a full understanding of the principle it contains.

b. It must contain correct focus of attention, use of power, good balance and proper breathing.

c. The performance should also be evaluated with a view to discerning other points.

Upon being called, the contestant will go directly to the competition area, stand on the designated line and bow to the judges. He will then announce clearly the *kata* he intends performing and start. On completion of the routine he will return to his mark and await the scoring. Upon completion of the routine the referee will call for a decision from the judges by blowing a whistle, at which point they will raise their appropriate scorecards.

There are one or two other questions that we may have left unanswered so the following chapter sets out to clear up those unanswered queries that will crop up from time to time.

The elbow (empi) is an invaluable contact point for striking your opponent forwards, sideways, backwards, upwards and downwards

Karate is not just about punching and kicking. The manoeuvring for position at the beginning of a bout is very important as both fighters endeavour to create an opening

Rules clinic

Competition karate is an exciting sport, conducted within a strict formula of rules. Here are the answers to some common questions to help you get started.

When does the timing of a contest begin?
From the moment the referee gives the call to start, *hajime*. The clock stops each time he calls *yame*.

Can a fighter score his three points to win a bout by obtaining six *waza-aris* (half points)?
Yes.

Is it possible to have a tied bout?
Yes. If neither fighter is ahead on points and the officials cannot decide the winner then the bout is a tie. Normally, an extra period of time (two minutes) will be allowed to find a winner. This is called *encho-sen*. The referee will commence this extra period with the call 'shobu hajime'.

Opposite: A good fighter needs to train regularly by practising not only kicks, strikes and blocks but also stance, balance and breathing

What happens if the scores are level at the end of, say, two minutes?
If the rules of the competition permit, 'extra time' will be allowed

and continue until the first score is made. If it were a penalty this would mean the guilty fighter would lose the contest. If the rules do not allow for an *encho-sen* the referee will award the contest to the fighter who he feels showed superiority based on his skill of technique, fighting spirit and a good attitude.

How many *karateka* normally take part in team matches?
Normally five, plus two reserves. There must be an odd number of fighters in each team.

If a bout goes into *encho-sen* do any penalties from the original part of the bout get deleted, or are they carried forward?
Sorry, but they're carried forward, because *encho-sen* is a continuation of the bout.

How is a team contest scored?
The number of victories is taken into consideration, and drawn matches remain drawn. The team with the most victories shall be deemed the victors. However, if they are level then points won by all fighters are accumulated and the team with the most points wins. Again, if the two teams are still level then a deciding bout will be held and the first fighter to be awarded an *ippon* or *waza-ari* shall win the match for his team. If they are still level after three minutes' fighting, an extension (*encho-sen*) will be allowed. If they are then still level, the officials will announce a winner based on the number of good techniques delivered and fighting spirit.

If both fighters land a blow simultaneously which one scores the point(s)?
Neither. They cancel each other out and the referee will call *ai-uchi*, which means 'simultaneous'.

If a scoring technique is delivered at the same time as the end of the bout is signalled, does it still score?
Yes. However, if it is delivered after time has been called it shall not score and may result in a penalty being called.

You have said that the throat, groin, instep, etc are forbidden contact areas. But what happens if I make contact with, say, my

opponent's throat, as a result of him unbalancing himself and falling on to me?
Naturally you will not be penalized.

Likewise, if I am propelled out of the fighting area by my opponent, does this count as a *jogai* against me?
Again, no.

If a fighter has so many *hansoku-chuis* and *keikokus* against him that they add up to a *sanbon* is he disqualified?
Yes. He will have *hansoku* called against him.

If a contest is interrupted before the end of its duration, is time allowed for this stoppage?
Yes. The clock is stopped the moment the contest is halted.

Are fully focused contact blows of any description permitted?
Yes, just one – the sweeping of your opponent's leg to knock him to the ground. This must, however, be followed by a controlled punch or kick in order to score.

If a fighter comes into the arena incorrectly or inappropriately dressed, is he disqualified?
Not automatically. He has one minute in which to rectify the situation.

What happens if you do step outside the fighting area and deliver a point-winning technique, does it count?
Once outside the match area, any point-winning technique is auto-matically declared invalid.

Can a fighter still be penalized after the completion of a bout?
Yes. Penalties can be imposed by the referee at any time up to the contestants leaving the fighting area. Even after that penalties can be imposed for such things as ungentlemanly conduct.

Let's say two fighters injure each other simultaneously and neither can continue fighting, how is the outcome decided?
The fighter leading on points at the time of the stoppage shall be

declared the winner. If the points are level then a decision (a *hantei*) will decide the bout.

What happens after each scoring blow?

The referee, judge and fighters return to their respective marks in the centre of the fighting area. The referee then announces either *ippon* or *waza-ari* to the appropriate fighter followed by the call of *'tsuzukete hajime'*, which means 'carry on'.

Apart from stopping the bout as a result of a point-scoring technique, when is the referee likely to call *'yame'* to stop the bout?

Well, it can be for any one of several reasons. The following are the most likely:

a. When one or both fighters are out of the fighting area.
b. When one fighter's *karategi* needs adjusting.
c. When a fighter appears to be about to break one of the rules.
d. When a fighter has broken the rules.
e. When one or both fighters need medical attention.
f. When one or both contestants fall or are thrown, and no effective technique follows.

Are there any rules about the wearing of jewellery when fighting?

Yes. You must not wear metallic or other objects which might injure your opponent or yourself. You mustn't have long fingernails either. Spectacles are also outlawed, I'm afraid, but soft contact lenses are permitted.

What happens in the event of a tie in a *kata*?

You remember earlier we said that the highest and lowest scores are discounted. Well, in the event of a tie then the minimum score is incorporated into a fighter's score for that round. If still level, then the maximum score is incorporated. In the event of a continued tie then the contestants must perform another *kata* of their choice.

Is it possible to be disqualified from a *kata*?

Yes. Disqualification follows if you interrupt or vary a routine or perform a *kata* different from the one drawn or indicated.

The front kick (Mae-geri) is made with the knee raised high before the leg is straightened to carry out the kick

Technique

A trained *karateka* is able to transmit the muscular power of the whole body to a striking limb. Tremendous energy is thereby transferred to the target. To carry out such movements with maximum effect, use must be made of correct stance, breathing and timing.

The whole of the body, and in particular those bonier regions, can be used as weapons in karate. But even a single finger can be a powerful weapon, with lethal effect in the original days when it was used as an effective form of fighting.

Don't take up karate if your sole reason is to be the next Bruce Lee. But do take it up if you want to enjoy a pleasurable and disciplined form of unarmed combat.

At an early stage of your development as well as sparring you need to concentrate on performing *kata*. There is no sense in thinking you can progress in karate by practising only freestyle fighting (*kumite*). Initially your *kata*(s) will lack finesse, but you will gradually build up confidence as you get more experienced.

Before we go into the various techniques we ought to reiterate that karate is about more than just scoring successful punches or kicks to various parts of your opponent's body.

'Good form' is a phrase that is crucial to good and effective karate. The technique has to be carried out with maximum effect within the framework of karate concepts and ideals. Correct attitude is one such component of 'good form'. Too many people take up karate with an over-eager and aggressive attitude but karate is not meant for those people. Your attitude should be of the non-malicious kind and great concentration and self-control are required in making sure that your scoring techniques do not harm your opponent.

Another characteristic of 'good form' is the vigorous application which defines the power and speed of the technique coupled with the insatiable desire to succeed with the technique.

And the final component of 'good form' is *zanshin*, the state of total awareness, even after the execution of a scoring technique. The *karateka* should always be aware of counter-attacks. That is where good *zanshin* is called for.

Correct timing should also be considered when attempting a scoring punch or kick. To be timed correctly it must be executed so that it would have the greatest potential effect if it made contact with your opponent. Likewise the technique should be executed from a proper distance so that any punch, blow or kick will have the maximum effect. If you deliver a blow to an opponent who is moving away from you then it would not have the maximum effect and would therefore not warrant the awarding of an *ippon*.

Before moving on to specific types of technique, it is important to look at training techniques.

Some *dojos* will have *makiwara* (padded boards) for practising and developing kicking and punching techniques. They will also help toughen the contact points, although children should avoid doing constant impact training for obvious reasons. Other standard training equipment will include dumb bells for carrying out weight-training exercises, punch bags and specially weighted leg clamps for developing muscles. A container of sand or polystyrene balls is useful for practising driving techniques with the hands.

The basic training, comprising blocks, strikes and kicks, and on stance, balance, breathing and focus, is called *kihon*. It may be

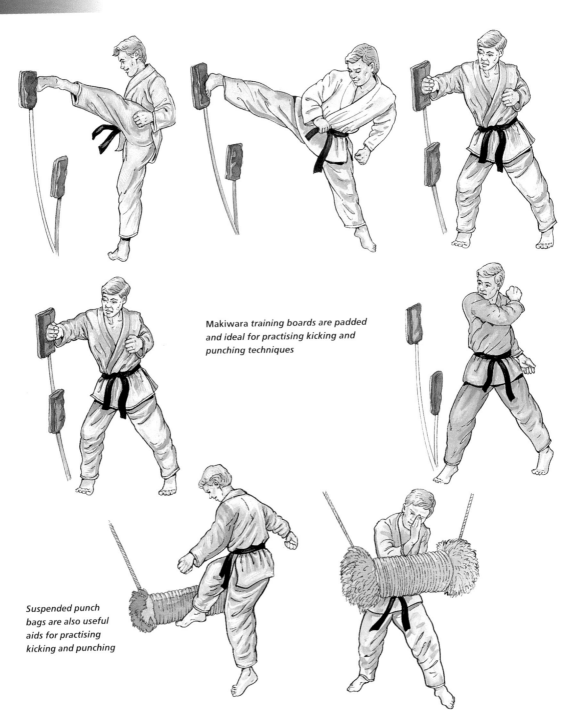

Makiwara *training boards are padded and ideal for practising kicking and punching techniques*

Suspended punch bags are also useful aids for practising kicking and punching

practised on your own or in groups. The latter is more enjoyable. When practised in groups, the instructor or the senior grade will lead the group, encouraging each fighter by example and by shouting commands to the rhythm of the practice.

PREPARATION

One of the first things to learn is how to stand properly, so now we will look at the different stances.

Stances

The various stances are designed for specific purposes. Those with a low centre of gravity and a wide foot stance are ideal for powerful punching, whereas others are designed for mobility and speed of technique. You should have a sound knowledge of the basic stances, which will be taught throughout your training.

     The *Zenkutsu-dachi* is one of those stances ideal for powerful punching. The centre of gravity is low, the feet are apart and the

The Zenkutsu-dachi *stance from the side (A) ...*
... and how it looks to your opponent (B)

A   B

THE FREESTYLE KAMAE *STANCE*
Most fighters will adopt a fluid stance based on the posture shown here. The fighter will be moving constantly, keeping up on his toes to manoeuvre for any advantage

body is very stable. It is a versatile stance from which both punches and kicks can be made with ease. In addition, most blocks and strikes can be made from this stance.

The term 'stance' however implies a fixed, rooted position. This can be misleading, as in modern freestyle fighting being rooted to the spot is very inadvisable. Sport karate requires that you are extremely athletic and mobile around the match area.

For freestyle purposes, most fighters adopt a *kamae* (or posture) that best suits their fighting style. The stance therefore becomes more flexible and may not even resemble any particular basic stance, but is perfectly adapted to the requirements of modern competition.

Generating power

If you look at a discus thrower or shot putter you will notice how power is generated as a result of a rotating movement of the body before the throw. The *karateka* generates power in the same way. The rotary movements of the *karateka* transmit velocity and power to the striking limb whether it be the arm or leg. These movements also help to unbalance your opponent.

Breathing

Part of the mental preparation of karate lies in the *karateka*'s ability to breathe properly and goes back to some of Zen's principles. The breathing patterns are designed to bring about a mental calm immediately prior to exploding into action and there are four distinct phases to each pattern:

a. Inhale through the nose until the lungs are full of air.

b. Force all the air downwards towards the diaphragm. You will not find this easy at first but after a bit of practice you will find you are transferring the air, and at the same time strengthening the muscles of the abdomen. The ability to breathe in the area of the abdomen and the use of the *kiai* help generate remarkable power.

c. Exhale quietly through the nose.

d. Finally, force the last remaining air out of your lungs.

Warming up

Don't forget to warm up when you first enter your training hall. There is nothing worse than starting any strenuous exercise from cold. Karate is certainly no different. Place some emphasis on stretching exercises to protect your muscles and improve their suppleness. Without any reasonable level of suppleness many kicks are impossible to carry out. Some useful warming-up exercises are illustrated on pages 52–4.

Kime (focus)

As already explained, a trained *karateka* is able to deliver destructive power to a target. This is achieved by the co-ordinated use of large muscle groups, breathing and timing. The *karateka* generates power by initiating movement at great speed and allowing a striking limb to accelerate in a ballistic fashion. Upon striking the target, all muscles are then briefly but forcefully contracted, which transmits all the available power to the target.

Before we go on to techniques, you ought to familiarize yourself with the points of your body that are designated 'contact points', that is those parts which are acceptable in scoring techniques. These are given on pages 55–9.

GENERATING POWER
You can see how the turning of the hips can add more power into this kick

**WARMING-UP
EXERCISES**

Warming up exercises are important. Ten to fifteen minutes stretching using a full routine will be of great benefit

Three more good stretching exercises (A–C)

A

This exercise will help you get your back supple and ready for karate actions

B

C

Both these exercises are crucial to the good karateka. Ensure your feet stay on the ground and use your stomach muscles to lift yourself into a sitting position

This is a very good exercise for strengthening your back and thigh muscles – you should really be able to feel them stretch

The contact points

The forefist (*Seiken*) Contact is made with the knuckles of the first and middle fingers of the clenched fist. Make sure the fist is well secured because the tighter the fist, the firmer the wrist.

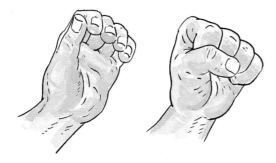

THE FOREFIST (SEIKEN)
To create a good forefist bend your fingers inwards and tightly grip the first two fingers with your thumb. Don't tuck your thumb under the fingers

The back fist (*Uraken*) This is employed when striking to the side of the head. The hand is closed tightly, as in the forefist (*Seiken*).

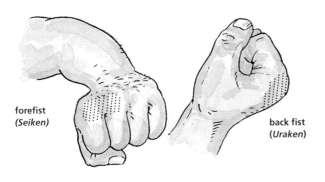

forefist
(*Seiken*)

back fist
(*Uraken*)

THE FOREFIST AND THE BACK FIST
The grip of the fingers for the back fist (Uraken) is similar to the forefist (Seiken) but the wrist is slightly bent this time

The spearhand (*Nukite*) Very useful when attacking soft parts of your opponent's body, such as the throat. Make sure your thumb is bent inwards. The contact point is the middle three fingers.

contact point
for striking

THE SPEARHAND (NUKITE)
An important 'weapon' when attacking those softer parts of your opponent's body. The contact is made with the tips of the three middle fingers so you will have to bend your middle finger slightly to position them in line

The wrist (*Koken*) The actual contact point is that part of the lower arm between your wrist and palm of the hand. This is used in attacks to the face and, sometimes, stomach. Make sure your wrist is well bent and out of the way so you can make contact with that boned part of the hand as outlined. The wrist is also used in blocks.

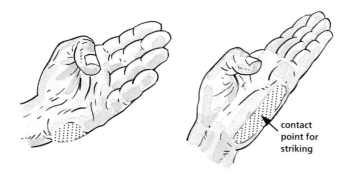

contact point for striking

THE WRIST (KOKEN)
Ideal in striking. The contact point is the base of the palm immediately before the wrist. The wrist is also used in blocking, in which case the back of the wrist can also be used

The knifehand (*Shuto*) Make sure your thumb is bent inwards otherwise you could sustain a nasty injury. As well as being a useful attacking aid, the knifehand is also invaluable for blocking.

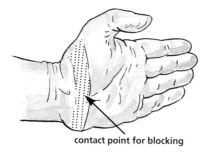

contact point for blocking

THE KNIFEHAND (SHUTO)
A useful contact point for both blocking and attacking. It is important that you bend your thumb inwards

The single-knuckle fist (*Ippon ken*) Only the middle knuckle is extended and the fingertip of your first finger is held securely.

THE SINGLE-KNUCKLE FIST (IPPON KEN)
The fist is clenched tightly and the middle knuckle is extended

THE ELBOW (EMPI)
The elbow is a versatile contact point

The elbow (*Empi*) A versatile contact point because you can use it to strike from any direction: forwards, sideways, upwards, downwards and even backwards.

Important: the spearhand, knifehand, single-knuckle fist and elbow attacks are particularly dangerous – so much so that they are not allowed in competition. Practise them very carefully.

Now for the legs and feet:

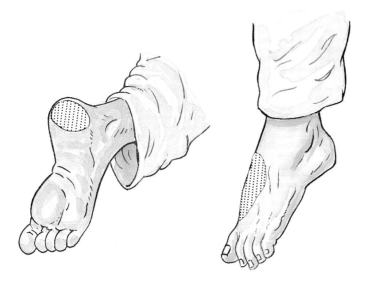

Far left: *THE HEEL* (KAKATO)
Used for backward kicks, stamping or thrusting

Left: *THE INSTEP* (HAISOKU)
Keep the toes extended. The instep is used for roundhouse kicks

The heel (*Kakato*) This contact point is used for backward kicks, thrusting or stamping kicks.

The instep (*Haisoku*) Used more often than not for roundhouse kicks to the head but can also be used for kicks to the groin. Keep the toes extended.

THE BALL OF THE FOOT (CHUSOKU) This time keep your toes bent upwards. It is the ideal contact point for front kicks, and occasionally roundhouse kicks

The ball of the foot (*Chusoku*) Also used in roundhouse kicks as well as for front kicks. Keep your toes well bent upwards.

THE KNIFE FOOT (SOKUTO) Ideal for side kicks

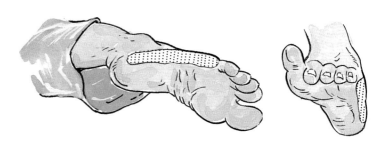

The knife foot (*Sokuto*) This contact point utilizes the outside of the foot and is used mainly in side kicks.

THE KNEE (HIZA)
The knee can also be an effective contact point in karate

The knee (*Hiza*) Yes, the knee is a good contact point, particularly into your opponent's stomach.

Note that in a karate competition you do not make an attack with any open-hand technique or with the elbow or knee.

Don't forget, we have already said that almost any boney part of the body can be used as a weapon (for example the single finger). The aforementioned are the most widely used, but don't feel you are restricted to them.

TECHNIQUES

Now for some punching and kicking techniques which will be looked at from two views – those of the attacker and those of the defender. You will need to learn how to combat attacking moves as well as making them.

This skill is acquired through exhaustive, pre-arranged sparring drills. One fighter looks for an opening in order to attack while the other evades this attack and, if successful, attempts to build up a counter-attack. The tactical battle is the one whereby the two fighters look for that first opening.

There are three ways of attacking: punching, kicking and sweeping. But as the last is for the more advanced fighter we are not going to give it a great deal of space in this book. Initially you will need to learn to develop only the first two skills.

Punching Unlike boxing, where the fighters are generally weaker with one hand than the other, the *karateka* needs to be an expert with both hands. If you can punch equally well with both hands then you have more chance of catching your opponent unaware. While kicking techniques look more attractive to the newcomer it cannot be emphasized too strongly that you also need to practise and develop punching techniques. And what is more, if you find that, say, your right hand is far superior to your left at punching, then you must spend time practising punching with your left hand.

Kicking The advantage of kicking over punching is the fact that you can put more space between yourself and your opponent, thus reducing the risk of a quick counter-attack. He can still counter-attack if your kick is a no-scoring one, but you will have more time to defend yourself.

PUNCHING TECHNIQUES
The front jab *(Kizami-zuki)*
Target Area:
The face

Attacking:
One of the basic punches, it is very little different to the jab in boxing. It is effective for opening up your opponent's defence. For example, you can use it to compel your opponent to block and counter. Anticipating the nature of the counter, you will then be able to block and immediately launch your own decisive counter-attack. Used as a feint in this way, the *kizami-zuki* can invoke a reactional response from your opponent that they will find difficult

THE FRONT JAB (KIZAMI-ZUKI)
Place your weight on your front foot to gain the maximum reach

to resist. Speed of thrust is important, both in executing the jab and, if unsuccessful, in retreating the arm and fist. Use of a hand-held striking pad in training is good exercise for the front jab.

Defending:

To spot the front jab coming keep an eye on your opponent. If he moves closer to you rapidly it is likely that a front jab is on its way. From your own stance position you should sweep with your

COUNTERING THE FRONT JAB
Your opponent may give a clue that he is about to punch by moving quickly forward (A). Be alert, and sweep his attacking arm away with your left arm and be ready to counter-attack with your right (B)

A

B

forearm and deflect the punch. The swivelling of the hips helps with the defensive movement. But after preventing the attack, you must be ready to counter-attack, probably with your other hand.

The back fist (*Uraken*)

Target Area:
Side of the head

Below: THE BACK FIST (URAKEN)
From a side-on position (A), with your elbow pointing at your opponent's face, straighten your attacking arm to carry out the successful back fist (B)

Bottom: COUNTERING THE BACK FIST
Note how the attacking left arm of the fighter on the right is deflected (C), and how the other fighter quickly attacks with a punch (D)

A

B

C

D

Attacking:

Similar to the front jab but this time the blow is with the back of the hand. It is used more as a counter-attack and requires quick hands.

Defending:

The back fist is a difficult strike to spot because you're never sure whether it is going to be a front jab or back fist. However, quick reactions are essential and if you move your head out of the way, it will bring your left upper arm upwards and ready to take the force of the punch. At the same time your opponent's middle area will be exposed and if you can recover your balance quick enough, and be alert enough, you can counter to that area.

The reverse punch *(Gyaku-zuki)*

Target Area:

Head and upper body from waist upwards, excluding the arms/neck

Attacking:

It is similar to the front jab but this time the damage is caused by the back hand as opposed to the front hand. The punch is made more powerful and effective by twisting your hips as you turn to make the punch. Because the fist has farther to travel than in the front jab you have to be very quick, or alternatively make sure you have a good opening otherwise you will find the punch blocked.

THE REVERSE PUNCH (GYAKU-ZUKI)
Rotating the hips adds extra power, reach and speed to the reverse punch

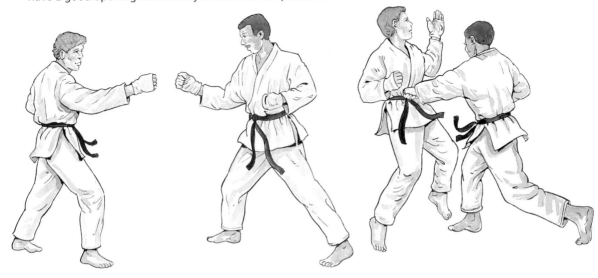

COUNTERING THE REVERSE PUNCH
*Being able to move sideways is
important in countering the reverse
punch. Make sure your opponent's
arm is deflected to the side and then
quickly swivel your hips to come in
with a counter-attack*

Defending:
You will have more time to spot the reverse punch, which can be deflected with your forearm. Be ready to counter-attack.

The roundhouse punch (*Mawashi-zuki*)

Target Area:
Side of the face

**THE ROUNDHOUSE PUNCH
(MAWASHI-ZUKI)**
This punch is so-called because it is made in a circular rather than a straight direction. Contact is with the forefist

Attacking:
This punch is distinct in that it travels in a circular path rather than in the straight one that most other punches do. You lunge forward with your left arm from the stance position and then rapidly bring forward the right fist into your opponent's face.
Defending:
Blocking would be similar to that for the front jab.

KICKING TECHNIQUES
The front kick (*Mae-geri*)
Target Area:
Stomach/upper abdomen

Attacking:
This is the first kick you will learn. Many novices believe the contact point is the toes. It is not. The contact point is the ball of the foot. To carry out an effective, point-scoring front kick you must ensure

THE FRONT KICK (MAE-GERI) This is a useful kick for smaller fighters matched against taller opponents because they can get under the taller person's guard

that your knee is lifted high enough and, using the power of the hips, your leg is then straightened to carry out the kick. You should not use a sweeping kicking movement from the floor into your opponent's stomach.

COUNTERING THE FRONT KICK Defending and counter-attacking the front kick require a good quick action moving from one side to the other. The first is to deflect the attacking leg and the second to deliver the counter-attack

Defending:

Side-step the kick and sweep the attacker's leg away with your front arm from a normal stance position. Your other arm should then be free for the counter-attack. And don't forget, you should have the advantage after a block because your opponent will be off-balance.

The roundhouse kick (*Mawashi-geri*)

Target Area:

Head, stomach or back

THE ROUNDHOUSE KICK (MAWASHI-GERI)
'Eyeing up' an opponent before deciding on what form of attack to adopt – in this case the roundhouse kick (A). Note how the attacker is leaning back as she prepares to execute the kick (B)

In the roundhouse kick the instep is used to make contact with your opponent

Attacking:

Like the front kick, the roundhouse kick depends on good twisting of the hips. The knee should also be lifted high before execution of the kick. The roundhouse is a spectacular kick and if perfected well can – like any well-delivered technique – get you a full point (*ippon*). The instep is used in the roundhouse kick. The ball of the foot can be used but, because it is dangerous, there is an 'unwritten' law amongst *karateka*s that says only the instep is used. The roundhouse kick to the face calls for perfect balance and your trunk should be at right angles to the standing leg. The reverse roundhouse *(Ushiro-mawashi-geri)* is made with the ball of the foot contacting your opponent's cheek bone. Like all roundhouse kicks, speed is important, and the transference of the feet from stance position to kicking position should be in one continuous movement.

Defending:

The most effective defence is by stepping forward from your normal stance and dropping your left arm to block with, but making sure you take the force of the kick on the muscle, not the elbow. If you keep your other elbow high it gives you the opportunity to counter-attack with, say, a back fist. The block against a roundhouse kick to the face lends itself to a perfect counter-attack

COUNTERING THE ROUNDHOUSE KICK
The roundhouse kick is defended by brushing aside the attacking leg of your opponent and then quickly twisting your hips to deliver your counter-strike

because your opponent will be off-balance and with his back to you. To counter a roundhouse kick to the face you must sweep your opponent's kicking leg out of the way. This will have the effect of turning him around.

The back kick (Ushiro-geri)

Target Area:

Abdomen

THE BACK KICK (USHIRO-GERI)
Timing, speed and accuracy are
important with the back kick

Attacking:

Regarded as the most powerful kick in karate. It is made more
lethal by the turning of the body as you turn into the kick. It is
effective if carried out properly but the big problem is the fact that

A

COUNTERING THE BACK KICK
*The quick 'one-two' is employed yet
again when defending the back (or
side) kick. The attacking leg is brushed
aside (A) and, again, the hips are
swivelled to enable the counter-punch
to be made (B)*

B

you turn your back on your
opponent to make the kick.
Defending:
Blocking is done by thrusting
downwards with the front arm on
to the opponent's kicking leg. The
counter-attack is made quickly with
the other arm.

The side kick
(*Yoko-geri*)
Target Area:
Chest/stomach

Attacking:

This time the power of the kick comes from the thrusting of the leg
rather than twisting of the hips. A very high knee position is
essential and the power is generated from that position as the leg is

THE SIDE KICK (YOKO-GERI)
*Timing, balance and keeping an eye
on your opponent are three vital
ingredients with the side kick ...*

*... but you must also execute it
correctly, and a very high knee
position at the start of the move is
important*

straightened. It can be effective if your opponent is near to the edge of the competition area because, if it doesn't score you a point, it may well carry a penalty for him if he steps off the mat.
Defending:
The kick is defended against in the same way as the back kick.

Those are the fundamental punches and kicks which you should try and develop. Don't forget, you will be penalized if they are landed with too much force. And remember, one of the keys to successful karate is being able to control the punch or kick after getting through your opponent's defence.

BLOCKING TECHNIQUES

Next we will look a bit closer at blocking because it is a very useful part of the *karateka*'s repertoire. Good blocking will prevent a successful attack from your opponent and at the same time set up your counter-attack. Many top international fighters are expert counter-attackers, letting their opponent do the work to begin with.

Blocking usually takes two forms. It can either be a blow to an attacking limb or a simple deflection. As a general rule, punches that are made to the head should be deflected upwards, those to the body should be deflected sideways, and those to the groin area should be deflected downwards.

SIDEWAYS BLOCK
From a forward stance the forearm block is very effective and with a sweeping movement of the right arm blocks your opponent's attack

DOWNWARD BLOCK
The downward block is ideal against kicks or punches to the stomach or abdomen region

CROSS BLOCKING
Cross-blocking techniques are rarely seen at competitive level but are still a useful form of defence

In addition to the single arm blocks as outlined in the techniques already described there are two-handed cross blocks with, as the name implies, the arms crossed. They are used in basic sparring as a defence of the face.

We have already mentioned the *kata* and it is important that you use this as your starting point. All *katas* start with a defensive move followed invariably by an attacking move. In some instances the defensive and attacking moves are similar and thus are designed to confuse your opponent when involved in a *kumite* contest.

When taking part in *kumite* fighting you will find it essential to string together a series of attacks, blocks, counter-attacks, and so on. This is where a good *kata* comes in useful as you put together a series of combination moves which will all go towards making you a better fighter. However, you must always remember that there is a good chance your attacking punch or kick will be blocked. Unless you are ready with your contingency attack then you will lose the advantage. So, be alert at all times. No matter what discipline you are carrying out you must always learn to keep your eyes on your opponent at all times and remember a good strong *kiai* (shout) counts towards winning points.

Finally, a brief mention of *tamashiwara* (wood-breaking), the spectacular aspect of karate and the one which many uninitiated believe is the only form of karate. In truth, very few *karateka* practise wood-breaking. However, its practice takes in the most widely taught of karate's principles: each fighter should empty his or her mind of all thoughts.

During a bout (kata), each fighter must constantly manoeuvre for the best position in which to create an opening

THE FRONT KICK/FRONT JAB COMBINATION
The front kick has been blocked but on regaining balance the front jab has been employed

Tamashiwara is, in effect, the combination of everything the karateka has already learned: discipline and strength. Unlike kata and kumite, where the karateka cannot display his feats of strength, tamashiwara allows him to show all of his skills. But many regard this branch of karate as the showmanship side of the sport.

The striking parts of the body used in tamashiwara require tremendous strength and power, but this power can be obtained only once the fear of striking something hard has gone. That is the spiritual aspect of karate. For the time being forget about tamashiwara and concentrate on your punching and kicking techniques.

Timing, speed and accuracy are of paramount importance in karate

THE BACK FIST/BACK LEG ROUNDHOUSE COMBINATION
The back leg roundhouse is employed after the back fist has been blocked

Useful
addresses

Karate Union of Great Britain
PO Box 3
Wirral L43 6XX
0151-652-1208

English Karate Governing Body
58 Bloomfield Drive
Bath
Somerset BA2 2BG
01225-834008

Northern Ireland Karate Association
3rd floor, 35 College Street
Belfast BT1 6BU
01232-616453

Scottish Karate Board Governing Body
2 Strathdee Road
Netherlee
Glasgow G44 3TJ
0141 633-1116

Welsh Karate Federation
Smalldrink
Parsonage Lane
Begelly
Kilgetty
Pembrokeshire
01834-813776

World Union of Karate-do Organizations
Senpaku Sinko Building
1–15–16 Toranoman
Minatu-Ku
Tokyo 105
Japan
00813-503-6638
or
122 Rue de la Tombe Issoire
75014 Paris
France
0033-143-95-42-00

Rules clinic
index

Page numbers *in italics* indicate illustrations

index

Figures *in italics* indicate illustrations

A Ward Lock Book • Cassell • Wellington House • 125 Strand • London WC2R 0BB

A Cassell Imprint • Copyright © Ward Lock 1998
All rights reserved. No part of this book may be reproduced or transmitted in any form or by any means,
electronic or mechanical, including photocopying, recording or any information storage and retrieval system,
without prior permission in writing from the publishers and copyright owner.

Distributed in the United States by • Sterling Publishing Co. Inc. • 387 Park Avenue South • New York NY 10016 • USA

British Library Cataloguing-in-Publication Data • A catalogue record for this book is available from the British Library

ISBN 0-7063-7714-1

Designed by Grahame Dudley Associates • Illustrations by Chris Rothero • Text revisions by Bryan Evans

Printed and bound in Spain by Graficromo S.A., Cordoba